ANIMAL NOSES

David M. Schwartz *is an award-winning author of children's books, on a wide variety of topics, loved by children around the world.* Dwight Kuhn's *scientific expertise and artful eye work together with the camera to capture the awesome wonder of the natural world.*

For a free color catalog describing Gareth Stevens Publishing's list of high-quality books and multimedia programs, call 1-800-542-2595 (USA) or 1-800-461-9120 (Canada). Gareth Stevens Publishing's Fax: (414) 225-0377.

Library of Congress Cataloging-in-Publication Data

Schwartz, David M.
    Animal noses / by David M. Schwartz; photographs by Dwight Kuhn.
       p. cm. — (Look once, look again)
    Includes bibliographical references and index.
    Summary: Describes the ways in which certain animals, such as snakes, dogs, weevils, moths, elephants, and owls, use their noses to pick up scents and breathe.
    ISBN 0-8368-2578-0 (lib. bdg.)
    1. Nose—Juvenile literature. [1. Nose. 2. Smell. 3. Senses and sensation. 4. Animals—Physiology.] I. Kuhn, Dwight, ill. II. Title. III. Series: Schwartz, David M. Look once, look again.
QL947.S35 2000
573.8'77—dc21   99-048370

This North American edition first published in 2000 by
Gareth Stevens Publishing
1555 North RiverCenter Drive, Suite 201
Milwaukee, Wisconsin 53212 USA

First published in the United States in 1998 by Creative Teaching Press, Inc., P. O. Box 6017, Cypress, California, 90630-0017.

Text © 1998 by David M. Schwartz; photographs © 1998 by Dwight Kuhn. Additional end matter © 2000 by Gareth Stevens, Inc.

Printed in the United States of America

1 2 3 4 5 6 7 8 9 04 03 02 01 00

ANIMAL NOSES

by David M. Schwartz
photographs by Dwight Kuhn

A SPRINGBOARDS INTO
SCIENCE
SERIES

Gareth Stevens Publishing
MILWAUKEE

Stay away
from this nose!

5

A snake breathes through nostrils at the front of its head. Some snakes also have small holes below the nostrils. These are heat-sensing pits, with which the snakes sense the warmth of small animals nearby.

Everyone knows this cold, wet nose.

You probably know how it feels on your hand or face.

7

Dogs are great sniffers. Their noses can find scents that people cannot smell. Some dogs use their noses to find lost or trapped people.

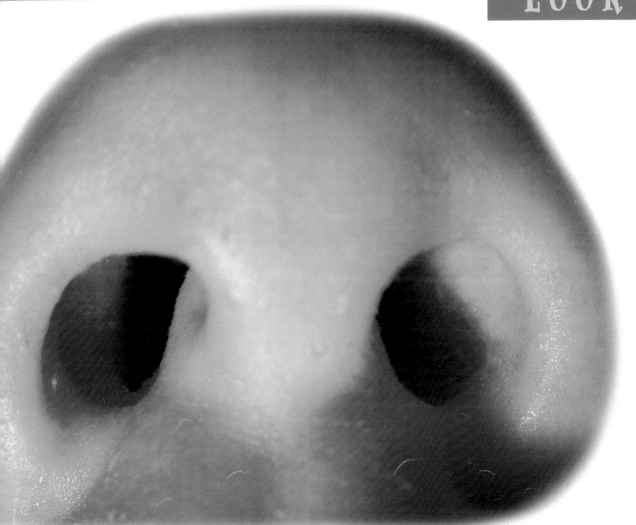

This nose
should be
very familiar
to you.

You use your nose to breathe and to smell things. It warns you when there is a fire, and it allows you to enjoy the scent of flowers.

This is one big nose!
No wonder the insect is
called a "snout beetle."

LOOK AGAIN

This insect is a weevil. It has a long snout with an antenna located on each side and sharp jaws at the tip. The antennae smell and feel objects. The weevil feeds on crops, such as cotton, rice, and wheat.

Are these giant
feathers on legs?

LOOK AGAIN

No. They are the feathery antennae of the luna moth.

The moth uses its antennae like a nose. A male luna moth can pick up the scent of a female from miles away.

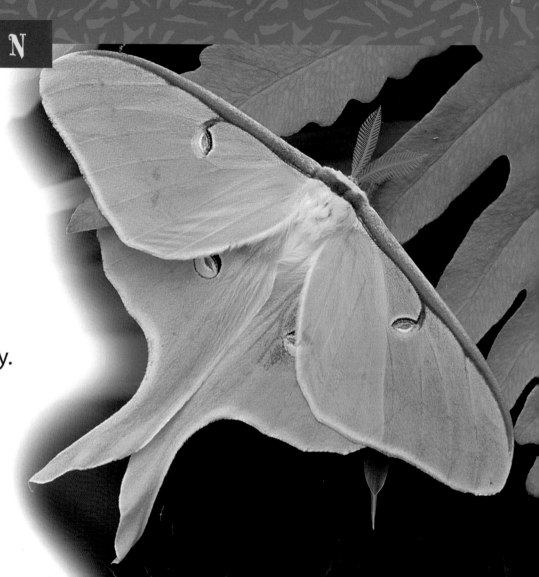

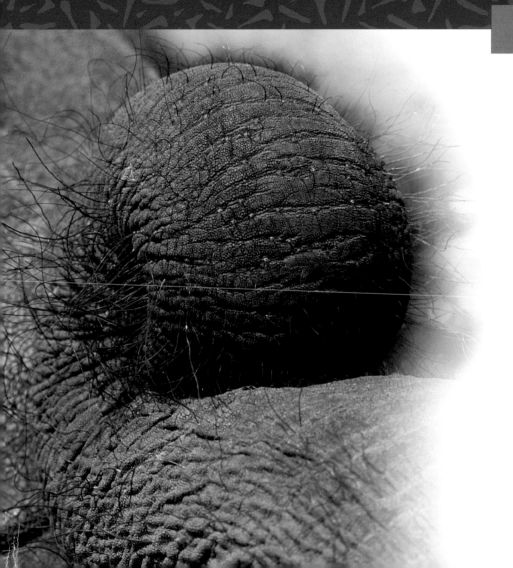

This is the longest nose of all. It is also a trunk that can bend, curl, or roll in any direction.

15

An elephant uses its trunk to breathe and smell. With its trunk, an elephant also puts food and water into its mouth and sprays water onto its back.

An elephant uses its trunk to rip branches from trees and to gently stroke its newborn calf.

This is a beak and also a nose. Whose nose could it be?

17

It is the hooked beak of the barred owl. The two small holes near the top of the beak are nostrils.

The owl breathes through its nostrils. Scientists do not know, however, if it can pick up scents through them.

A.

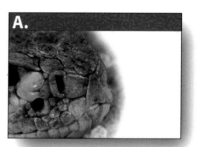

B.

C.

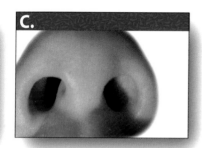

D.

E.

F.

G.

Look closely. Do you know to which animals these noses belong?

A.

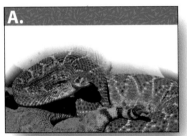

Rattlesnake

B.

Dog

C.

Human

D.

Weevil

E.

Luna moth

F.

Elephant

G.

Barred owl

How many were you able to identify correctly?

antenna: one of a pair of "feelers" located on the head of insects.

barred: the state of having alternate bands of different colors.

beak: the jaws of a bird that have a hornlike covering; a bird's bill.

beetle: an insect that has four wings.

calf: the young of certain large animals, such as cows, whales, elephants, and buffalo.

crops: a large quantity of plants that are grown for an income.

familiar: something that is known.

heat-sensing pits: receptors that allow certain snakes to sense warm-bodied prey.

insect: a small animal with three pairs of legs, one or two sets of wings, a head, a thorax, and an abdomen.

jaws: the bones in the mouth that hold the teeth.

moth: a four-winged insect that usually flies at night.

nostrils: the fleshy walls of the nose.

owl: a nocturnal bird of prey with large eyes, a hooked beak, and talons.

scents: smells, aromas.

snout: a long, projecting nose.

trunk: the elongated, muscular nose of the elephant.

ACTIVITIES

What's That Smell?

Can you sometimes tell what something is before you actually see it just by your sense of smell? Can you tell who people are by the smell of their perfume? Can you smell cookies baking in the oven? Can you smell popcorn when you go to the movies? Can you recognize unpleasant smells, too, such as the spray of a skunk or cigarette smoke? Make a list of some of the objects you can recognize by smell. Label them as pleasant or unpleasant.

Nosy Expressions

Make a list of expressions that people use involving the nose, such as "She has a nose for news," "He is nosy," and "Nose your way through the crowd." What do you think is meant by each of those expressions? Can you think of others? What do they mean?

Field Trip

Visit a zoo. At the zoo, you'll see many different animals with many different noses. In a notebook, write down the name of the animal, followed by the type of nose it has. When you return home, group together the animals that have similar noses. What do members of each group have in common? How are the groups different from each other?

Nose to the Rescue!

Search the Internet for news stories about dogs that sniff out drugs, that search for people in need of rescue, or that do detective work for police departments. What kind of contributions have these dogs made to society? What kind of training did they undergo? What were their lives like before they were chosen for this type of work?

More Books to Read

Animal Opposites (series). Barbara J. Behm (Gareth Stevens)
Animal Senses. Animal Survival (series). Michel Barré (Gareth Stevens)
Breathtaking Noses. Hana Machotka (Morrow)
Owl Magic for Kids. Animal Magic for Kids (series). Neal D. Niemuth (Gareth Stevens)
Sammy: Dog Detective. Colleen S. Bare (Dutton)
The Science of Insects. Living Science (series). Janice Parker (Gareth Stevens)
The Science of Senses. Living Science (series). Patricia Miller-Schroeder (Gareth Stevens)

Videos

Animal Senses. (DK Publishing)
Animals Breathe in Many Ways. (Phoenix/BFA)
How the Elephant Got His Trunk. (Coronet)

Web Sites

www.pbs.org/wishbone/index.html
206.63.59.98/Mammals/Proboscidea/5.htm

Some web sites stay current longer than others. For further web sites, use your search engines to locate the following topics: *beaks, elephants, noses, owls, rattlesnakes,* and *weevils.*

INDEX